American Gen Z Dictionary

Definitions and Explanations of Modern Slang

J.D Quillian

Table of Contents

Introduction

What is Slang?

Ever feel like people are speaking a different language online? You're not entirely wrong. It's called slang, and it's been around for ages, constantly reinventing itself with each generation. Slang is informal language used by a particular group of people. It's like a secret code, a way to signal belonging and shared experiences. Think of it as the ever-evolving, super-casual cousin of standard language.

Slang is characterized by a few key things:

Informality: Slang thrives in casual settings—text messages, social media, hanging out with friends. You wouldn't use it in a formal presentation (unless you're really trying to make a point).

In-Group Use: Slang acts as a social marker, creating a sense of community among those who use it. It can be a way to identify with a particular subculture, age group, or online community.

Evolving Nature: Slang is constantly changing. What's "in" today might be "cheugy" (more on that later) tomorrow. This rapid evolution is especially true in the digital age, where trends spread like wildfire online.

For Gen Z, slang is more than just casual talk; it's a vital part of our identity. It reflects our experiences, humor, and the unique ways we interact with the world, especially online. It's how we express ourselves creatively, connect with each other, and shape online culture.

Generational Differences:

Generations are groups of people born around the same time who share similar cultural experiences and historical events:

Silent Generation (born roughly 1928-1945): Grew up during the Great Depression and World War II. Known for their work ethic and traditional values.

Baby Boomers (born roughly 1946-1964): Experienced post-war prosperity and social change. Known for their activism and focus on individual achievement.

Generation X (born roughly 1965-1980): Grew up during a time of economic uncertainty and shifting social norms. Often described as independent and cynical.

Millennials (born roughly 1981-1996): Came of age in the digital era and experienced the Great Recession. Known for their tech-savviness and social consciousness.

Generation Z (born roughly 1997-2012): Grew up with the internet and social media. Known for their diversity, digital fluency, and focus on social issues.

Generation Alpha (born roughly 2013-2025): The first generation born entirely in the 21st century. Growing up in an increasingly digital and interconnected world.

Each generation has its distinct slang, reflecting the times they live in.

Why This Dictionary?

The internet moves fast, and Gen Z slang moves even faster. Trying to keep up can feel like chasing a runaway train. That's where this dictionary comes in. It's your essential guide to navigating the ever-changing landscape of Gen Z lingo.

This dictionary is crucial because:

Gen Z slang evolves rapidly: New terms pop up daily, making it difficult for anyone outside the loop to understand what's being said.

Context is key: Understanding Gen Z slang requires more than just knowing the definition of a word; it's about understanding the cultural context in which it's used.

It bridges generational gaps: This dictionary isn't just for Gen Z; it's for anyone who wants to better understand how we communicate. Parents, teachers, older siblings, and anyone curious about online culture will find this resource invaluable.

It unlocks online culture: From memes to TikTok trends, slang is deeply intertwined with online culture. This dictionary will help you decipher the language of the internet and participate more fully in online conversations.

Scope and Criteria/How to Use

This dictionary focuses specifically on American Gen Z slang—terms commonly used in the United States by people roughly born between 1997 and 2012. We've included words and phrases that are frequently used online and in everyday conversations, demonstrating clear cultural relevance.

Dictionary Entry Format:

Each entry will follow this format:

Headword: The slang term itself.

Pronunciation (if necessary): A phonetic guide to help you pronounce the word correctly.

Definition: A clear and concise explanation of the term's meaning.

Example: A sentence or short dialogue demonstrating the term in context.

We hope this dictionary serves as a useful and engaging resource for anyone looking to understand the unique language of Gen Z. Get ready to decode the digital dialect!

A

And I oop-

And I oop- (and eye oop) interjection

1. An expression of surprise, shock, or mild embarrassment, often used when something unexpected or slightly clumsy happens to oneself or someone else. It conveys a sense of playful self-deprecation or amusement at a minor mishap.

2. Can also be used as a reaction to something cute, exciting, or surprising, similar to "Oh my gosh!" or "Oops!" but with a more exaggerated and playful tone.

Example 1: I was walking down the stairs and tripped, and I oop- almost fell!

Example 2: She just announced she's engaged! And I oop- so happy for her!

Originating from a viral video featuring Jasmine Masters, a contestant on RuPaul's Drag Race, the phrase became popular on social media, particularly among LGBTQ+ communities and then spread into wider Gen Z usage. It's often accompanied by a hand gesture mimicking a dramatic gasp or a hand over the mouth. While initially associated with minor accidents, its meaning has broadened to express a range of surprised or excited reactions. It emphasizes a lighthearted reaction to a situation. Synonyms include "Oops," "Oh no," "Oh my gosh," or "Whoops," but and I oop- adds a more dramatic and humorous flair.

Ate

Ate (ayt) verb (past tense of eat, used colloquially)

1. Used to express that someone (or something) performed exceptionally well, excelled in a particular area, or completely "killed it" or "slayed" (in a positive sense). It implies a high degree of success, skill, or impact. It's often used in the context of performances, fashion, or other forms of self-expression.

2. Often used with the phrase "left no crumbs," further emphasizing the thoroughness of the success.

Example 1: Beyoncé ate that performance; the vocals were insane!

Example 2: Her outfit for the Met Gala ate and left no crumbs. Everyone was talking about it.

This usage of "ate" is a figurative extension of the literal meaning of consuming something completely. The idea is that the performer or creation "consumed" the competition or the moment, leaving nothing behind. It's a hyperbole used to express extreme approval and admiration. It is a derivative of Black Vernacular English (BVE) that has crossed over into mainstream Gen Z slang, particularly through online platforms like TikTok and Twitter. Related terms include "slay," "kill it," "smash," or "crush it," but "ate" has a particularly strong connotation of effortless excellence and dominance. It emphasizes not just doing well, but doing so with style and impact.

Adulting

Adulting (uh-dult-ing) verb (gerund)

1. The practice of behaving in a way considered typical of adult life, often involving mundane tasks and responsibilities such as paying bills, grocery shopping, doing laundry, or maintaining a job.

2. Often used humorously or ironically to express the challenges, frustrations, or unexpected difficulties of navigating everyday adult life. It can also convey a sense of accomplishment for completing a particularly "adult" task.

Example 1: I spent all weekend adulting—doing laundry, cleaning the apartment, and meal prepping for the week.

Example 2: I finally managed to file my taxes without any help. I feel like I'm really adulting today!

While the term "adulting" has been used by previous generations, it gained significant popularity among Millennials and Gen Z, particularly on social media platforms. It reflects a shared experience of going through the often-unprepared-for realities of adulthood, especially in the context of economic challenges and delayed milestones. The term often carries a tone of lighthearted complaint or self-deprecation, acknowledging the less glamorous aspects of being an adult. It can also be used to celebrate small victories in managing adult responsibilities. There aren't direct synonyms, but related concepts include "adult responsibilities," "grown-up stuff," or "the daily grind," though these lack the specific connotation of humorous struggle or ironic accomplishment that "adulting" conveys.

AF (as f***)

AF (as f) (ay-eff) adverb/intensifier

Used as an intensifier to emphasize the degree or extent of something. It is a more emphatic version of "very" or "really." Due to the inclusion of the expletive, it is considered informal and often used in casual settings or online communication.

Example 1: This pizza is good AF.

Example 2: I'm tired AF after that workout.

The abbreviation "AF" is a shortened form of "as f***." The word "f***" is a common expletive in English, and its use as an intensifier has become widespread in informal contexts. While the full phrase is considered vulgar by some, the abbreviation "AF" is often seen as less offensive and has become more widely accepted, especially in online communication. Related intensifiers include "very," "really," "extremely," or "super," but "AF" carries a stronger, more emphatic connotation. It is important to note that its use might be considered inappropriate in formal settings.

Aggro

Aggro (ag-roh) adjective/noun

1. **Adjective:** Short for "aggressive" or "aggravated." Used to describe someone or something that is behaving in a hostile, confrontational, or agitated manner.

2. **Noun:** Short for "aggression." Refers to aggressive behavior or a state of being agitated.

Example 1 (Adjective): He got really aggro when the referee made that call.

Example 2 (Noun): There was a lot of aggro in the crowd after the game.

"Aggro" is a shortening of the word "aggressive" and has been used in various subcultures for many years, including sports and music scenes. Its use has become more widespread within Gen Z through online gaming communities and social media. Synonyms include "aggressive," "hostile," "confrontational," "agitated," or "antagonistic." The use of "aggro" often implies a sense of low-level tension or simmering anger, rather than outright violence.

All good

All good (awl good) phrase/interjection

1.   Used to express that everything is okay, fine, or satisfactory. It can be used as a response to an apology, an expression of concern, or a general inquiry about someone's well-being.

2.   Can also be used to dismiss something minor or to indicate that there are no hard feelings.

Example 1: "Sorry I'm late." "It's all good."

Example 2: "Did you get the email?" "Yeah, all good."

"All good" is a common phrase in informal English, and its usage within Gen Z is consistent with general usage. It's a casual and reassuring way to confirm that everything is fine. Synonyms include "okay," "fine," "no problem," "no worries," or "it's alright." "All good" often implies a sense of ease and informality.

Ambitious

Ambitious (am-bish-uhs) adjective (used ironically)

Used ironically to describe something that is clearly mundane, unremarkable, or even slightly absurd. It's used to create a humorous contrast between the grand connotation of "ambitious" and the reality of the situation.

Example: I'm going to try to finish this entire bag of chips in one sitting. I know, I'm so ambitious.

This ironic usage of "ambitious" is a way to express self-deprecating humor or to playfully mock the trivial nature of certain goals or activities. It highlights the gap between aspiration and reality. There aren't direct synonyms for this ironic usage, but it's related to concepts like "overly optimistic," "pretentious," or "grandiose," but with a more lighthearted and humorous tone.

Anxiety

Anxiety (ang-zy-uh-tee) noun (often used hyperbolically)

While "anxiety" has its standard definition relating to a mental health condition, it is often used hyperbolically by Gen Z to describe feelings of nervousness, stress, or worry, even in relatively minor situations. This usage can sometimes downplay the seriousness of clinical anxiety, which is important to be mindful of.

Example: I have so much anxiety about this test tomorrow, even though I studied.

This hyperbolic use of "anxiety" reflects the prevalence of stress and worry in contemporary society, particularly among young people. It's important to differentiate between this casual usage and clinical anxiety, which is a serious mental health condition. While not a direct synonym, related terms in this hyperbolic context include "stressed," "worried," "nervous," or "freaked out." It's crucial to be sensitive to the potential trivialization of mental health when using "anxiety" in this way.

B

Bet

Bet (bet) interjection/adverb

1. **Interjection:** Used as an affirmation, agreement, or confirmation. It expresses certainty or willingness to do something. Similar to "Okay," "Sure," "Deal," or "I agree."

2. **Adverb**: Used to express certainty or emphasis, similar to "definitely" or "for sure."

Example 1 (Interjection): "Want to grab some food later?" "Bet."

Example 2 (Adverb): I'm bet going to pass this test.

"Bet" originates from African American Vernacular English (AAVE) and has become widely adopted in mainstream Gen Z slang. It conveys a casual and confident tone.

Basic

Basic (bay-sik) adjective

Used to describe someone or something that is conventional, unoriginal, or mainstream to the point of being considered boring or uninteresting. It often implies a lack of individuality or unique taste.

Example: Her outfit is so basic—leggings, Uggs, and a North Face jacket.

"Basic" gained popularity in the early 2010s and has remained a common term in Gen Z slang. It's often used with a slightly negative or dismissive connotation, but can also be used playfully.

Bae

Bae (bay) noun

A term of endearment for a romantic partner or significant other. It can also be used more generally for someone you find attractive or close to.

Example: I'm going to the movies with my bae tonight.

"Bae" is thought to be a shortening of "baby" or possibly derived from Danish. It became popular in the early 2010s and is still widely used.

Bop

Bop (bop) noun/verb

1. **Noun: A** catchy or enjoyable song, especially one that makes you want to dance.

2. **Verb:** To move or dance to music, especially in a lively or energetic way.

Example 1 (Noun): This song is a total bop!

Example 2 (Verb): We were bopping all night at the party.

"Bop" has been used in various contexts for decades, but its current usage within Gen Z is specifically associated with enjoyable music.

Boujee/Bougie

Boujee/Bougie (boo-zhee) adjective

Describing something or someone that is luxurious, fancy, or high-class, often in a way that is perceived as pretentious or trying too hard.

Example: This restaurant is so bougie—look at the prices!

"Boujee" is derived from the word "bourgeois." It can be used both positively and negatively, depending on the context and the speaker's intent.

Big Mad

Big Mad (big mad) adjective

Extremely angry or upset. It emphasizes a strong degree of anger or frustration.

Example: He was big mad when he found out he failed the test.

"Big mad" is a more emphatic version of "mad" or "angry." It conveys a heightened emotional state.

Bussin'

Bussin' (buh-sin) adjective

Used to describe food that tastes exceptionally good or delicious.

Example: This burger is bussin'!

"Bussin'" is believed to have originated within Black communities and has gained popularity through social media, especially TikTok. It's a highly positive descriptor for food.

Broke

Broke (brohk) adjective (often used ironically)

While "broke" has its standard definition of lacking money, it is often used ironically by Gen Z to describe situations where someone is experiencing minor inconveniences or temporary financial constraints.

Example: I can't buy that extra coffee; I'm broke (because I already bought one).

This ironic usage of "broke" is a way to playfully exaggerate minor financial issues.

Bestie

Bestie (bes-tee) noun

A close friend or best friend.

Example: I'm going shopping with my bestie this weekend.

"Bestie" is a shortened and more affectionate version of "best friend."

Big yikes

Big yikes (big yikes) interjection

An expression of strong disapproval, embarrassment, or awkwardness. It emphasizes a particularly uncomfortable or cringeworthy situation.

Example: He just asked her out in front of everyone, and she said no. Big yikes.

"Big yikes" is a more emphatic version of "yikes." It conveys a heightened sense of discomfort or embarrassment.

C

Cap (No Cap)

Cap (No Cap) (kap/noh kap) noun/interjection

Noun: A lie or exaggeration. The term alludes to the idea of wearing a "cap" or hat, symbolizing something that is not true or genuine.

Interjection ("No Cap"): Used to emphasize that what one is saying is true and not a lie or exaggeration. It serves as a declaration of honesty and authenticity.

Example 1 (Noun): That story he told was pure cap. There's no way that actually happened.

Example 2 (Interjection): I won the lottery, no cap. I'm serious!

The origin of "cap" in this context is debated, with potential roots in Black slang and hip-hop culture. The phrase "no cap" gained widespread popularity on social media platforms like TikTok and Twitter. It's a way to distinguish between factual statements and fabricated ones, adding a layer of emphasis to claims of truthfulness. Synonyms for "cap" (as a noun) include "lie," "falsehood," "exaggeration," or "fabrication." The phrase "no cap" can be compared to "for real," "seriously," "honestly," or "I'm not kidding." The use of "no cap" often suggests a desire to be perceived as genuine and transparent, especially in online interactions where it can be difficult to discern truth from fiction.

Caught in 4k

Caught in 4k (kot in for kay) phrase/interjection

Used to describe a situation where someone has been caught doing something embarrassing, incriminating, or otherwise compromising, usually with clear video or photographic evidence (4k resolution video). It implies that the evidence is undeniable and of high quality, leaving no room for denial.

Example: He was caught in 4k cheating on the test because someone filmed him looking at his neighbor's paper.

"4k" refers to a high-definition video resolution (3840 x 2160 pixels), implying a very clear and detailed recording. The phrase emphasizes the indisputable nature of the evidence. The phrase gained popularity with the rise of social media platforms where videos and photos can easily go viral. It's often used humorously to describe even minor embarrassing moments, but can also refer to more serious situations. Related phrases include "busted," "caught red-handed," or "exposed," but "caught in 4k" specifically highlights the presence of high-quality visual evidence. The use of "4k" adds a contemporary and tech-savvy element to the phrase.

Certified

Certified (ser-ti-fahyd) adjective

Used to describe something or someone that is undeniably excellent, authentic, or of high quality. It implies that something has met a certain standard or has been officially recognized as being exceptional.

Example: This song is a certified banger. Everyone's listening to it.

"Certified" in this context is a figurative extension of its standard meaning, which refers to something that has been officially verified or documented. Its usage in Gen Z slang is often associated with music, particularly songs that are considered hits or have achieved significant popularity. It can also be applied to other things, such as fashion, skills, or even people. It implies a high level of approval and recognition. Synonyms include "legit," "authentic," "genuine," "top-tier," or "undeniable," but "certified" carries a particular connotation of official recognition or widespread acclaim. It emphasizes that the quality is not just a matter of opinion, but rather a widely accepted fact.

Chill

Chill (chil) adjective/verb/noun

1. Adjective: Relaxed, calm, or easygoing.

2. Verb: To relax, unwind, or spend time casually.

3. Noun: A relaxed or calm atmosphere or state of mind.

Example 1 (Adjective): He's a really chill guy.

Example 2 (Verb): We're just chilling at home tonight.

Example 3 (Noun): There's a really good chill vibe here.

"Chill" has been used in various contexts for many years, but its usage within Gen Z is consistent with its established meanings. It's a versatile word that can be used to describe a person, a situation, or an activity. Synonyms include "relaxed," "calm," "laid-back," "easygoing," or "mellow." The word "chill" is often associated with informal settings and social gatherings. It emphasizes a lack of stress or pressure.

Clout

Clout (klout) noun

Influence or social power, often gained through online presence, popularity, or connections. It refers to the ability to influence others or attract attention and recognition.

Example: He's got a lot of clout on social media because he has millions of followers.

"Clout" has been used for many years to refer to influence or power, but its specific association with online influence has become more prominent within Gen Z. It's often associated with social media influencers and online celebrities. The pursuit of "clout" can sometimes be seen negatively, implying a focus on superficial popularity or attention-seeking behavior. Related terms include "influence," "prestige," "reputation," "status," or "pull," but "clout" specifically emphasizes the ability to attract attention and exert influence in online spaces.

Cringe

Cringe (krinj) verb/adjective/noun

1. Verb: To recoil or shrink back in embarrassment or disgust.

2. Adjective: Causing feelings of embarrassment or awkwardness.

3. Noun: A feeling of embarrassment or awkwardness.

Example 1 (Verb): I cringed when he told that awkward joke.

Example 2 (Adjective): That video is so cringe. I can't even watch it.

Example 3 (Noun): I got the cringes watching that scene.

"Cringe" has been used for many years to describe a physical reaction of recoiling or shrinking back. Its usage in Gen Z slang extends to describe feelings of social awkwardness or embarrassment, often in response to observing someone else's behavior. It's a common reaction to online content that is perceived as awkward, try-hard, or embarrassing. Related terms include "embarrassed," "awkward," "uncomfortable," or "mortified." The use of "cringe" often implies a strong sense of vicarious embarrassment.

Curve

Curve (kurv) verb/noun

1. Verb: To reject someone romantically or platonically, often in a subtle or indirect way.

2. Noun: An act of rejection.

Example 1 (Verb): She tried to ask him out, but he curved her.

Example 2 (Noun): He gave her a hard curve by ignoring her texts.

The origin of "curve" in this context is believed to stem from the idea of swerving or changing direction to avoid something. It implies a gentle or indirect form of rejection, rather than a direct and harsh refusal. The term gained popularity through online dating and social media. Synonyms include "reject," "turn down," "rebuff," or "dismiss," but "curve" often implies a more subtle or less confrontational form of rejection. It can also suggest an attempt to avoid hurting someone's feelings.

Cancelling

Cancelling (kan-sel-ing) verb (present participle)

Referring to the practice of withdrawing public support for someone or something, usually a celebrity, brand, or public figure, after they have done or said something considered offensive or problematic. It often involves boycotts, social media backlash, and attempts to damage their career or reputation.

Example: That celebrity was cancelled after their racist tweets resurfaced.

"Cancelling" has become a prominent term in recent years, particularly in discussions about social justice and accountability. It reflects a desire to hold people and organizations responsible for their actions and words. The practice of "cancelling" can be controversial, with debates about its effectiveness, fairness, and potential for misuse. Related terms include "boycott," "ostracize," "shun," or "deplatform," but "cancelling" specifically implies a public withdrawal of support and an attempt to damage someone's reputation or career. It often involves social media campaigns and online activism.

D

Drip

Drip (drip) noun/adjective

1. Noun: Stylishness, especially in clothing and accessories. Refers to a fashionable and attractive appearance, often associated with expensive or trendy items.

2. Adjective: Stylish, fashionable, or cool.

Example 1 (Noun): He's got serious drip with that new outfit.

Example 2 (Adjective): That jacket is so drip.

The term "drip" originated in hip-hop culture and has become widely adopted by Gen Z. It emphasizes a strong sense of personal style and confidence. The imagery is of water "dripping" off something, implying an abundance or excess of style. Synonyms include "style," "swag," "fashion," "flair," or "look." The use of "drip" often suggests a high level of attention to detail and a desire to impress. It can also imply a degree of extravagance or luxury.

Dead

Dead (ded) adjective/interjection

1.   Adjective: Used hyperbolically to express extreme amusement, shock, or disbelief. Similar to "dying" or "I can't."

2.   Interjection: Used as an exclamation of extreme amusement or shock.

Example 1 (Adjective): That joke was so funny, I'm dead.

Example 2 (Interjection): Dead! I can't believe that just happened.

"Dead" in this context is a figurative extension of its literal meaning. It's a hyperbole used to express a strong emotional reaction, often in a humorous way. It doesn't literally mean that someone has died. Synonyms include "dying," "I can't," "I'm done," "I'm weak," or "I'm deceased," all of which express similar levels of amusement or shock. The use of "dead" is often accompanied by laughter or other expressions of amusement.

Down Bad

Down Bad (doun bad) adjective

Used to describe someone who is experiencing intense romantic longing, desperation, or obsession, often to a self-deprecating or humorous degree. It implies a strong desire for someone's affection or attention, sometimes to the point of behaving irrationally.

Example: He's been texting her nonstop; he's down bad.

"Down bad" is a relatively recent addition to Gen Z slang. It's often used with a tone of playful mockery or commiseration. It acknowledges the sometimes-uncomfortable or embarrassing feelings associated with strong romantic desire. There aren't direct synonyms, but related concepts include "obsessed," "infatuated," "lovesick," "smitten," or "thirsty," although "down bad" carries a stronger connotation of desperation or irrational behavior.

Dope

Dope (dohp) adjective

Used to describe something that is cool, awesome, excellent, or impressive.

Example: That new song is dope.

"Dope" has been used as slang for "good" or "cool" for decades, originating in the early 20th century. Its continued use within Gen Z is consistent with its established meaning. Synonyms include "cool," "awesome," "great," "excellent," "amazing," or "fantastic." "Dope" is a versatile term that can be used to describe a wide range of things, from music and fashion to experiences and events.

Delulu

Delulu (Delusional) (di-loo-loo/di-loo-zhuh-nl) adjective

Short for "delusional." Used to describe someone who is holding onto unrealistic or unfounded beliefs or hopes, often in a humorous or self-aware way. It acknowledges a disconnect between reality and someone's perception of it.

Example: I know he doesn't like me, but I'm being delulu and still hoping he'll ask me out.

"Delulu" is a shortened and more casual version of "delusional." It's often used in a lighthearted or self-deprecating manner, acknowledging one's own tendency to engage in wishful thinking. It gained popularity on social media platforms like TikTok. Synonyms include "delusional," "unrealistic," "out of touch with reality," or "living in a fantasy world," but "delulu" carries a more playful and less harsh connotation.

Dis

Dis (dis) verb/noun

1. Verb: To disrespect or insult someone, often in a subtle or indirect way. Short for "disrespect."

2. Noun: An act of disrespect or an insult.

Example 1 (Verb): He totally dis'ed me by ignoring my text.

Example 2 (Noun): That was a major dis.

"Dis" is a shortening of "disrespect" and has been used in various subcultures for many years. Its continued use within Gen Z is consistent with its established meaning. Synonyms include "disrespect," "insult," "offend," "belittle," or "slight." "Dis" often implies a deliberate attempt to undermine someone's status or self-esteem.

DMs

DMs (Direct Messages) (dee-emz) noun

Private messages sent directly between users on social media platforms.

Example: I'll send you the details in the DMs.

"DMs" is a common abbreviation used across various online platforms. It's a convenient way to refer to private communication. The use of "DMs" is not unique to Gen Z, but it is a standard term within their online communication. Related terms include "private messages," "PMs," or "inbox messages." The use of "DMs" emphasizes the private nature of the communication, as opposed to public posts or comments.

E

Extra

Extra (ek-struh) adjective

Used to describe someone or something that is excessively dramatic, over-the-top, or attention-seeking. It implies a behavior or style that is beyond what is considered normal or necessary.

Example: She wore a full ball gown to the casual dinner; she's so extra.

"Extra" in this context is a figurative extension of its standard meaning of "additional" or "more than what is usual." It's often used with a slightly negative or critical connotation, but it can also be used playfully or humorously. The term gained popularity on social media and is often associated with reality television and online personalities. Synonyms include "dramatic," "over-the-top," "excessive," "theatrical," or "overdoing it." The use of "extra" often implies a desire for attention or a lack of self-awareness. It can also be used to describe a particularly flamboyant or exaggerated style.

E-boy/E-girl

E-boy/E-girl (ee-boi/ee-gurl) noun

Terms used to describe a specific subculture or aesthetic that emerged online, particularly on platforms like TikTok and Tumblr. They are characterized by a distinct style of dress, makeup, and online persona.

E-boy: Typically characterized by dark clothing, often with stripes or chains, dyed hair (often black or bright colors), and eyeliner. They often cultivate a melancholic or edgy online persona.

E-girl: Typically characterized by winged eyeliner, blush on the nose and cheeks, dark or brightly colored hair, and often wear oversized T-shirts, striped long sleeves, or other alternative fashion. They often cultivate a cute or quirky online persona.

Example: He's got the full e-boy look with the chain and the black nail polish. She's rocking the e-girl aesthetic with her heart stamps and oversized hoodie.

The "E" in "E-boy" and "E-girl" stands for "electronic," referring to their strong online presence. The subculture is heavily influenced by internet culture, including anime, gaming, and alternative music. While the terms were initially used to label a specific group, they have also become broader descriptors for a particular aesthetic. The terms have faced criticism for sometimes being used in a stereotypical or dismissive way.

Era

Era (as in "in my...") (eer-uh) noun

Used to describe a specific period in someone's life, often characterized by a particular style, interest, or set of experiences. The phrase "in my..." is used to introduce the description of this period.

Example: In my "emo era," I only wore black and listened to My Chemical Romance.

This usage of "era" is a figurative extension of its standard meaning of a historical period. It's used to create a sense of nostalgia or to reflect on a distinct phase of one's life. The phrase "in my..." emphasizes personal experience and ownership of that period. It often implies a significant change or shift in one's identity or interests. There aren't direct synonyms, but related concepts include "phase," "period," "stage," "time," or "chapter." The use of "era" adds a sense of importance or significance to the described period, suggesting that it was a formative or defining time. It is often used in a self-reflective or humorous way, acknowledging past trends or phases.

F

Finna

Finna (fin-uh) contraction

A contraction of "fixing to," meaning "going to" or "about to." It indicates an immediate or near-future action.

Example: I'm finna go to the store.

"Finna" originates from African American Vernacular English (AAVE) and has become widely adopted in mainstream Gen Z slang, particularly through online platforms and music. It's a casual and informal way to express intention. While grammatically non-standard in formal English, it is a common and accepted part of informal communication among many young people. Synonyms include "going to," "about to," "intending to," or "getting ready to," but "finna" has a more casual and immediate connotation.

Fit

Fit (fit) noun

Short for "outfit." Refers to a person's clothing and overall appearance.

Example: I love your fit today!

"Fit" is a shortened version of "outfit" and has been used in various subcultures for some time. Its use has become more widespread within Gen Z. It's a concise and casual way to refer to someone's attire. Synonyms include "outfit," "look," "ensemble," "attire," or "clothes." The use of "fit" often implies an appreciation for someone's style or fashion sense. It can also be used to describe a specific combination of clothing items.

Flex

Flex (fleks) verb/noun

1. Verb: To show off or boast about something, often in a boastful or ostentatious way.

2. Noun: An act of showing off or boasting.

Example 1 (Verb): He's always flexing his new car.

Example 2 (Noun): That was a serious flex.

"Flex" has been used for some time to refer to showing off physical strength or muscles. Its usage in Gen Z slang has broadened to include showing off possessions, achievements, or other forms of status. It often carries a slightly negative connotation of being boastful or arrogant, but it can also be used playfully or humorously. Synonyms include "show off," "boast," "brag," "flaunt," or "parade." The use of "flex" often implies a desire to impress others or to assert dominance.

Finsta

Finsta (Fake Instagram account) (fin-stuh) noun

A secondary or private Instagram account, often used to share content with a smaller, more trusted group of friends. It is typically used to post content that one might not want to share on their main, public Instagram account.

Example: I posted that embarrassing video on my finsta.

"Finsta" is a portmanteau of "fake" and "Instagram." It reflects the desire for a more private and unfiltered online presence. The use of finstas is common among young people who want to control who sees certain aspects of their lives. It allows for more casual or personal sharing without the pressure of maintaining a perfect public image. Related terms include "private account," "spam account," or "close friends list," but "finsta" specifically refers to a separate Instagram account used for this purpose.

FOMO

FOMO (Fear Of Missing Out) (foh-moh) noun

Anxiety or fear that one is missing out on social events, experiences, or opportunities.

Example: I have serious FOMO when I see everyone posting about the party I couldn't go to.

"FOMO" is an acronym that has become widely used in the digital age. It reflects the constant exposure to social media and the feeling of being connected to everything that is happening. It's a common experience among young people who are constantly bombarded with images and updates from their peers. There aren't direct synonyms, but related concepts include "anxiety," "worry," "jealousy," or "envy." The use of "FOMO" specifically highlights the fear of being excluded or left behind.

For real

For real (for reel) phrase/interjection

Used to express sincerity, agreement, or confirmation. It emphasizes that what one is saying is true or genuine.

Example 1 (Phrase): Are you for real? You actually won the lottery?

Example 2 (Interjection): For real! I'm not kidding.

"For real" is a common phrase in informal English, and its use within Gen Z is consistent with general usage. It's a casual and emphatic way to express truthfulness or agreement. Synonyms include "seriously," "honestly," "truly," "actually," or "no kidding." The use of "for real" often implies a desire to be believed or to emphasize the importance of what is being said.

G

Ghosting

Ghosting (goh-sting) verb/noun

1. Verb: To abruptly end all communication with someone without explanation, typically in a romantic or social context.

2. Noun: The act of abruptly ending communication with someone without explanation.

Example 1 (Verb): He ghosted me after our first date.

Example 2 (Noun): Ghosting is a really hurtful way to end a relationship.

"Ghosting" has become a widely recognized term in the digital age, particularly with the rise of online dating and social media. It describes a form of social rejection that is often perceived as rude and inconsiderate. It avoids direct confrontation or explanation, leaving the other person feeling confused and hurt. While not a new phenomenon, the term has gained significant prominence in recent years.

There aren't direct synonyms that fully capture the abrupt and unexplained nature of "ghosting," but related concepts include "ignoring," "avoiding," "cutting off," or "disappearing." The use of "ghosting" often implies a lack of empathy or respect for the other person's feelings.

Glow Up

Glow Up (gloh up) noun/verb

1. Noun: A significant improvement in one's appearance, style, or overall well-being.

2. Verb: To undergo a significant improvement in one's appearance, style, or overall well-being.

Example 1 (Noun): She had a major glow up over the summer.

Example 2 (Verb): He really glowed up after he started working out.

"Glow up" implies a transformation that is noticeable and positive. It can refer to physical changes, such as a new hairstyle or improved fashion sense, but it can also refer to personal growth, increased confidence, or improved mental health. The term gained popularity on social media, often accompanied by before-and-after photos. Synonyms include "transformation," "makeover," "improvement," or "upgrade." The use of "glow up" often conveys a sense of self-improvement and empowerment.

Go Off

Go Off (goh awf) verb

To express oneself with great energy, enthusiasm, or passion, often in a rant or outburst. It can also mean to perform exceptionally well or to do something impressive.

Example 1 (Expressing oneself): She really went off on him for being late again.

Example 2 (Performing well): The band went off during their concert.

"Go off" has been used in various contexts for some time, but its usage within Gen Z often emphasizes a strong emotional expression or a high level of performance. It can be used both positively and negatively, depending on the context. Synonyms for expressing oneself include "rant," "rave," "vent," or "express oneself strongly." Synonyms for performing well include "kill it," "smash it," "do amazing," or "excel."

Gucci

Gucci (goo-chee) adjective/interjection

1. Adjective: Used to describe something that is good, cool, excellent, or stylish, often associated with luxury or high quality.

2. Interjection: Used as an exclamation of approval or excitement.

Example 1 (Adjective): That car is Gucci.

Example 2 (Interjection): Gucci! We got the tickets!

"Gucci" is a reference to the high-end fashion brand. Its use as slang has broadened to encompass anything that is considered desirable or high-quality. It's often used with a sense of playful exaggeration or irony. Synonyms include "good," "cool," "great," "excellent," "amazing," "fancy," or "luxurious."

Gaslighting

Gaslighting (gas-lahy-ting) verb/noun

1. Verb: To manipulate someone into questioning their own sanity, memory, or perception of reality.

2. Noun: The act of manipulating someone into questioning their own sanity, memory, or perception of reality.

Example 1 (Verb): He was gaslighting her by denying that he had said those things.

Example 2 (Noun): Gaslighting is a form of emotional abuse.

"Gaslighting" originates from the 1938 play Gas Light and the subsequent film adaptations. It describes a form of psychological manipulation that is often used in abusive relationships. The term has gained wider recognition in recent years, particularly in discussions about domestic violence and emotional abuse. It's a serious term that describes a harmful and manipulative behavior.

GTG

GTG (Got To Go) (gee-tee-jee) abbreviation/interjection

An abbreviation for "Got To Go." Used to indicate that one needs to leave or end a conversation.

Example: GTG, I have to catch my bus.

"GTG" is a common abbreviation used in online communication and text messaging. It's a quick and concise way to excuse oneself from a conversation. Related abbreviations include "BRB" (Be Right Back), "TTYL" (Talk To You Later), or "AFK" (Away From Keyboard). The use of "GTG" is not unique to Gen Z, but it is a standard part of their online communication.

H

Highkey

Highkey (hahy-kee) adverb

Used to express something openly, obviously, or publicly. It signifies a strong and clear intention or feeling that is not hidden or concealed. It is the opposite of "lowkey."

Example: I highkey want to go to that concert.

"Highkey" is a relatively recent addition to Gen Z slang. It provides a way to express strong desires or opinions without any ambiguity. It emphasizes the openness and directness of the statement. While similar to "really," "definitely," or "obviously," "highkey" carries a stronger connotation of public declaration or open acknowledgment. It implies that the speaker is not trying to hide their feelings or intentions. It is often used in online communication and social media.

Hits different

Hits different (hits dif-er-uhnt) phrase

Used to describe something that evokes a strong emotional response or provides a unique experience that is noticeably different from similar things. It implies a qualitative difference that is difficult to articulate but easily felt.

Example: Listening to this song after a long day hits different.

"Hits different" is a phrase that gained popularity on social media, particularly on platforms like TikTok. It's used to express a nuanced and often subjective experience. It can be applied to a wide range of things, such as music, food, places, or even memories. The phrase emphasizes the distinctive and impactful nature of the experience. It suggests that the experience is not just good or enjoyable, but that it resonates on a deeper level. It is often used to describe experiences that are emotionally charged or that evoke strong feelings of nostalgia, joy, or sadness.

Hype

Hype (hahyp) noun/verb/adjective

1. Noun: Intense excitement or enthusiasm, often generated by marketing or promotion.

2. Verb: To promote or generate excitement for something.

3. Adjective: Excited or enthusiastic.

Example 1 (Noun): There's a lot of hype around the new movie.

Example 2 (Verb): They're really hyping up this new product.

Example 3 (Adjective): I'm so hyped for the concert tonight.

"Hype" has been used for many years to refer to promotional activity or inflated marketing. Its usage within Gen Z has broadened to encompass general excitement and enthusiasm. It can refer to anticipation for an upcoming event, excitement about a new product, or general enthusiasm for something. Synonyms for the noun include "excitement," "enthusiasm," "anticipation," or "buzz." Synonyms for the verb include "promote," "publicize," "advertise," or "generate excitement." The use of "hype" often implies a high level of energy and anticipation. It can also sometimes carry a slightly negative connotation of being overblown or exaggerated.

I

I'm Weak

I'm Weak (ahym week) phrase/interjection

An expression of extreme amusement or laughter, often in response to something funny or ridiculous. It is a hyperbolic statement, not meant to be taken literally.

Example: That meme was so funny, I'm weak!

"I'm weak" is a common expression in Black Vernacular English (BVE) that has crossed over into mainstream Gen Z slang. It's a figurative way of saying that something is so funny it has rendered one physically weak with laughter. It is similar in meaning to "I'm dying," "I can't," or "dead," all of which are hyperbolic expressions of amusement. The phrase is often used in online communication and social media, particularly in response to memes, jokes, or funny videos. It emphasizes the intensity of the laughter or amusement.

IYKYK

IYKYK (If You Know You Know) (if yoo noh yoo noh)
abbreviation/phrase

An abbreviation for "If You Know You Know." Used to indicate that a statement, joke, or reference is only understandable to a specific group of people who share a particular experience, inside joke, or piece of information. It creates a sense of exclusivity or shared understanding.

Example: That awkward moment in class today, IYKYK.

"IYKYK" is a common abbreviation used in online communication and social media. It's a way to acknowledge a shared experience without having to explain it to everyone. It reinforces a sense of belonging within a specific group. It can also be used to create intrigue or curiosity among those who don't understand the reference. The phrase is often used in captions on social media posts or in comments on online forums. It emphasizes the shared knowledge or experience of a select group.

It's giving...

It's giving... (its giv-ing) phrase

Used to describe the vibe, aesthetic, or energy that someone or something is projecting. It implies that something is evoking a particular feeling, style, or impression.

Example: Her outfit is giving major 80s vibes.

"It's giving..." is a relatively recent addition to Gen Z slang that has gained popularity on social media, particularly on platforms like TikTok and Twitter. It's a concise way to express a subjective impression or to describe a particular aesthetic. It can be applied to a wide range of things, such as fashion, music, art, or even personalities. The phrase emphasizes the overall feeling or impression that something is conveying. It is often used in a playful or descriptive way, adding a layer of nuance to the description. It is often followed by a specific descriptor, such as "main character energy," "old money," or "dark academia."

J

Janky

Janky (jang-kee) adjective

Describing something that is of poor quality, unreliable, or in bad condition. It can also refer to something that is makeshift, improvised, or poorly constructed.

Example: This old car is so janky; it barely runs.

"Janky" has been used in various contexts for some time, but its usage within Gen Z is consistent with its established meaning. It implies a lack of quality or craftsmanship. It can be applied to a wide range of things, such as objects, places, or even situations. Synonyms include "shoddy," "rickety," "flimsy," "broken-down," "poorly made," or "unreliable." The use of "janky" often conveys a sense of dissatisfaction or disapproval. It can also sometimes be used humorously to describe something that is endearingly imperfect.

Just saying

Just saying (juhst say-ing) phrase/interjection

Used to add emphasis to a statement or to express an opinion without being overly assertive or confrontational. It can also be used to imply a subtle criticism or suggestion.

Example 1 (Emphasis): That movie was really boring, just saying.

Example 2 (Subtle criticism): You might want to double-check your work, just saying.

"Just saying" is a common phrase in informal English, and its use within Gen Z is consistent with general usage. It's a way to express an opinion or observation without being overly forceful. It can also be used to soften a potentially critical statement. Synonyms include "I'm just saying," "I'm only saying," "I'm simply saying," or "I'm just pointing out." The use of "just saying" can sometimes be used sarcastically or ironically, depending on the context and tone of voice.

JOMO

JOMO (Joy Of Missing Out) (joh-moh) noun

The feeling of pleasure or satisfaction derived from disconnecting from social activities or online interactions. It is the opposite of FOMO (Fear Of Missing Out).

Example: I decided to stay home and read a book instead of going to the party; I was experiencing some serious JOMO.

"JOMO" is a relatively recent term that emerged as a counterpoint to FOMO. It reflects a growing awareness of the negative effects of constant connectivity and the desire to prioritize personal well-being and relaxation. It suggests that there is value in disconnecting and enjoying one's own company or engaging in solitary activities. The term gained popularity in discussions about digital wellness and mindfulness. There aren't direct synonyms, but related concepts include "contentment," "peace of mind," "relaxation," "solitude," or "enjoying one's own company." The use of "JOMO" emphasizes the positive aspects of disconnecting and prioritizing personal well-being.

K

Keep it 100

Keep it 100 (keep it wuhn-hundred) phrase/interjection

Used to express honesty, authenticity, or truthfulness. It emphasizes being genuine and real, without pretense or exaggeration.

Example: I'm keeping it 100 with you; that wasn't my best performance.

"Keep it 100" originates from Black Vernacular English (AAVE) and has become widely adopted in mainstream Gen Z slang. The "100" represents being completely truthful or authentic, as in 100% real. It's a way to emphasize sincerity and transparency. Synonyms include "being real," "being honest," "telling the truth," "being genuine," or "being authentic." The phrase often implies a desire to be open and upfront, even if the truth is difficult or uncomfortable.

KMS

KMS (Keep Myself Safe/Kill Myself) (kay-em-es) abbreviation

This abbreviation has two very different meanings, and it's crucial to understand the context to avoid misinterpretation and potential harm.

1. **Keep Myself Safe:** In this context, it expresses a desire for safety and well-being. It's often used in situations where someone feels vulnerable or threatened. This usage is less common than the other meaning.

2. **Kill Myself:** This is the more common and deeply concerning meaning. It expresses feelings of extreme distress, despair, or suicidal ideation. This usage should be treated with extreme caution and sensitivity.

Example 1 (Keep Myself Safe - less common usage): I'm walking home alone at night; I'm trying to KMS.

Example 2 (Kill Myself - more common and concerning usage): This test is so hard, I KMS. (This is often used hyperbolically but can also indicate genuine distress.)

It is essential to recognize that while "KMS" is often used hyperbolically to express frustration or stress, it can also be a cry for help. If someone uses "KMS" in a way that suggests genuine suicidal thoughts, it's crucial to take it seriously and offer support. Resources like crisis hotlines and mental health professionals should be recommended. Using "KMS" lightly can trivialize serious mental health struggles and should be avoided. This dictionary entry strongly advises against using "KMS" due to its potential for misinterpretation and the risk of minimizing serious mental health concerns.

Kinda

Kinda (kin-duh) adverb

Short for "kind of." Used to express a degree of uncertainty, approximation, or mildness. It softens or qualifies a statement.

Example: I'm kinda tired.

"Kinda" is a common contraction in informal English, and its use within Gen Z is consistent with general usage. It's a casual way to express a moderate degree of something. Synonyms include "kind of," "sort of," "somewhat," "slightly," or "a little bit." The use of "kinda" can sometimes indicate a lack of confidence or a desire to avoid being too direct.

L

Lit

Lit (lit) adjective

Used to describe something that is exciting, excellent, fun, or enjoyable. It can refer to a party, event, experience, or even a person.

Example: That party last night was lit.

"Lit" has been used as slang for "intoxicated" for some time, but its more recent usage within Gen Z has shifted to mean "exciting" or "enjoyable." It's a highly positive descriptor that conveys a strong sense of enthusiasm. Synonyms include "awesome," "amazing," "great," "exciting," "fun," or "epic." The use of "lit" often implies a high level of energy and excitement. It can also be used to describe something that is trendy or popular.

Lowkey

Lowkey (loh-kee) adverb/adjective

1. Adverb: Used to express something discreetly, subtly, or privately. It signifies a desire to keep something hidden or not to draw attention to it.

2. Adjective: Discreet, subtle, or private.

Example 1 (Adverb): I lowkey want to go to the beach this weekend.

Example 2 (Adjective): It was a lowkey gathering with just a few friends.

"Lowkey" is the opposite of "highkey." It provides a way to express desires or opinions without being overly assertive or public. It emphasizes the discreet or subtle nature of the statement. While similar to "secretly," "quietly," or "subtly," "lowkey" carries a stronger connotation of intentional concealment or a desire to avoid attention.

Living Rent-Free

Living Rent-Free (liv-ing rent-free) phrase

Used to describe something or someone that is constantly on one's mind, often in an annoying or intrusive way. It implies that the thought or person is occupying one's mental space without permission or payment (like living in a house without paying rent).

Example: That song has been living rent-free in my head all day.

"Living rent-free" is a relatively recent addition to Gen Z slang. It's a figurative way of expressing that something is persistently present in one's thoughts, often against one's will. It can refer to a song, a phrase, a memory, or even a person. The phrase emphasizes the involuntary and intrusive nature of the thought or presence.

L + Ratio

L + Ratio (el plus ray-shoh) phrase

Used in online arguments or disagreements to signify a loss or defeat. The "L" stands for "loss," and "ratio" refers to the number of replies or comments a post receives compared to the number of likes or retweets. A post with significantly more replies than likes/retweets is considered "ratioed," indicating that the post is unpopular or controversial.

Example: He made a really bad take on Twitter and got L + Ratio'd.

"L + Ratio" is a term that originated on Twitter and has become widely used in online spaces. It's a concise way to declare victory in an online argument or to indicate that a post has been widely criticized. The phrase emphasizes the social media metrics as a measure of success or failure.

LOL

LOL (Laughing Out Loud) (lol) abbreviation/interjection

An abbreviation for "Laughing Out Loud." Used to express amusement or laughter, often in online communication.

Example: That joke was hilarious! LOL.

"LOL" is an older internet slang term that is still used in some contexts, although it is often seen as less expressive than newer terms like "LMAO" or "I'm dead." It's a standard way to indicate amusement in online text-based communication.

LMAO

LMAO (Laughing My Ass Off) (el-em-ay-oh) abbreviation/interjection

An abbreviation for "Laughing My Ass Off." Used to express extreme amusement or laughter.

Example: I can't believe that happened! LMAO.

"LMAO" is similar to "LOL" but expresses a higher degree of amusement. It's a more emphatic way to indicate laughter. While considered vulgar by some due to the inclusion of "ass," it is a common part of informal online communication.

Lost

Lost (lost) adjective (as in "I'm lost")

Used to express confusion, disorientation, or a lack of understanding. It can refer to being physically lost or mentally confused.

Example: I'm lost in this new city. / I'm completely lost in this math problem.

While "lost" has its standard meaning, its usage within Gen Z is consistent with general usage. It's a common way to express confusion or a lack of comprehension. The phrase "I'm lost" is often used in online communication to indicate that someone needs help understanding something.

M

Mid

Mid (mid) adjective

Used to describe something that is mediocre, average, or unremarkable. It implies a lack of excitement, quality, or distinction.

Example: That movie was mid; it wasn't bad, but it wasn't great either.

"Mid" is a relatively recent addition to Gen Z slang. It's a concise way to express a neutral or slightly negative opinion. It doesn't necessarily mean something is bad, but rather that it is simply average or uninteresting. Synonyms include "mediocre," "average," "ordinary," "unremarkable," "so-so," or "meh." The use of "mid" often conveys a sense of indifference or mild disappointment. It can also be used humorously to downplay something that is slightly underwhelming.

Main Character

Main Character (mayn kar-uhk-ter) noun/adjective

1. Noun: Refers to someone who acts as if they are the central figure or protagonist in a story or movie, often exhibiting dramatic or attention-seeking behavior.

2. Adjective: Describing behavior or actions that are dramatic, attention-seeking, or characteristic of a main character.

Example 1 (Noun): She's such a main character; she always has to be the center of attention.

Example 2 (Adjective): He's giving main character energy with that dramatic entrance.

The concept of the "main character" is a figurative extension of the role of a protagonist in a narrative. Its usage in Gen Z slang often implies a self-centered or dramatic personality. It can be used both critically and playfully, depending on the context. Related terms include "dramatic," "attention-seeking," "self-centered," "theatrical," or "extra." The phrase "main character energy" is often used to describe someone who exudes confidence and charisma.

Mood

Mood (mood) noun/interjection

1. Noun: A state of mind or feeling. In slang usage, it often refers to a relatable feeling or situation that is widely shared.

2. Interjection: Used to express that something is relatable or resonates with one's current feelings.

Example 1 (Noun): Rainy days are my mood.

Example 2 (Interjection): This meme is such a mood.

"Mood" has been used for many years to refer to a state of mind. Its usage within Gen Z has broadened to encompass relatable feelings or situations that are often shared online. It's a concise way to express empathy or shared experience. The use of "mood" as an interjection is often accompanied by an image, video, or other piece of media that evokes the described feeling.

Meme

Meme (meem) noun

An image, video, text, or other item, typically humorous in nature, that is copied and spread rapidly by internet users, often with slight variations.

Example: I saw a funny meme about cats on the internet today.

"Meme" has become a widely recognized term in the digital age. It refers to a key form of online communication and cultural expression. Memes often reflect current trends, events, or social commentary. They can range from simple image macros to complex multimedia creations. The spread of memes is a key aspect of internet culture and online communities.

Mutuals

Mutuals (myoo-choo-uhlz) noun

Short for "mutual followers" or "mutual friends" on social media. Refers to people who follow or are friends with each other on the same platform.

Example: We have a lot of mutuals on Instagram.

"Mutuals" is a common term used in online social networking. It's a concise way to refer to shared connections. The existence of mutuals can often facilitate connections or introductions between people. The term emphasizes the shared network or community.

Mans

Mans (manz) noun (plural)

A plural form of "man," used informally to refer to a group of people, typically male. It can also be used more generally to refer to people regardless of gender.

Example: What are mans doing tonight?

"Mans" originates from various dialects and has become widely used in Gen Z slang. It's a casual and informal way to refer to a group of people. While traditionally associated with male groups, its usage has broadened to include mixed-gender groups or even general references to people. It is often used with a casual, friendly, or sometimes slightly humorous tone. The singular form "man" is less common in this context.

N

No Cap

No Cap (noh kap) interjection/phrase

Used to emphasize that what one is saying is true and not a lie or exaggeration. It serves as a declaration of honesty and authenticity. It's the opposite of "cap," which means a lie or exaggeration.

Example: I actually met my favorite celebrity yesterday, no cap.

"No cap" is a popular phrase that originated within Black slang and hip-hop culture and has become widely adopted by Gen Z. It's a way to distinguish between factual statements and fabricated ones, adding a layer of emphasis to claims of truthfulness. Synonyms include "for real," "seriously," "honestly," "I'm not kidding," "for sure," or "truly." The use of "no cap" often suggests a desire to be perceived as genuine and transparent, especially in online interactions where it can be difficult to discern truth from fiction. The phrase's popularity has spread across various social media platforms, solidifying its place in contemporary internet slang.

NPC

NPC (Non-Playable Character) (en-pee-see) noun/adjective

1. Noun: A character in a video game that is not controlled by a player. In slang usage, it refers to someone who is perceived as lacking individuality, agency, or independent thought, often conforming to social norms or trends without question.

2. Adjective: Describing someone who is perceived as lacking individuality, agency, or independent thought.

Example 1 (Noun): He just follows all the trends without thinking for himself; he's such an NPC.

Example 2 (Adjective): That's such an NPC thing to do.

"NPC" is a term borrowed from video game terminology. Its usage in Gen Z slang is often used critically or humorously to describe people who are perceived as conforming to stereotypes or lacking originality. The term can be seen as somewhat derogatory, implying a lack of depth or individuality. Related terms include "follower," "conformist," "sheep," "basic," or "mainstream." The use of "NPC" often reflects a desire for authenticity and individuality. It can also be used in self-deprecating humor to acknowledge one's own tendencies to conform.

NGL

NGL (Not Gonna Lie) (en-jee-el) abbreviation/phrase/interjection

Used to preface a statement, indicating that the speaker is being honest and truthful, even if the statement might be unpopular or controversial. It's a way to express candor or frankness.

Example: NGL, I didn't really enjoy that movie.

"NGL" is a common abbreviation used in online communication and text messaging. It's a concise way to introduce a potentially sensitive or controversial opinion. It signals that the speaker is being upfront and honest. Synonyms include "honestly," "frankly," "to be honest," "in all honesty," or "I'll be honest." The use of "NGL" often implies a desire for transparency and authenticity, even if the truth is difficult or uncomfortable. It can also be used to soften a potentially harsh statement by acknowledging its potential impact.

O

Oof

Oof (oof) interjection

An expression of discomfort, pain, surprise, or empathy. It can be used in response to a physical injury, an emotional setback, an awkward situation, or simply something unfortunate.

Example: I just tripped and fell in front of everyone. Oof.

"Oof" is an interjection that has gained widespread popularity online. It's a versatile expression that can convey a range of emotions, from mild discomfort to significant pain or embarrassment. It's often used in response to online content, such as memes or videos, that depict unfortunate or awkward situations. While the exact origin is unclear, it has become a staple of internet slang. There aren't direct synonyms that capture the same range of emotions, but related expressions include "ouch," "yikes," "uh oh," or "that's rough." "Oof" is often used with a tone of commiseration or empathy.

OK Boomer

OK Boomer (oh-kay boo-mer) phrase/interjection

A dismissive response used to reject or dismiss an opinion or viewpoint associated with the Baby Boomer generation (born roughly 1946-1964), often perceived as outdated, out of touch, or condescending.

Example: "Back in my day, we worked hard and didn't complain." "OK Boomer."

"OK Boomer" became a viral phrase in 2019, symbolizing generational conflict and differing perspectives on various social and political issues. It's often used in response to comments perceived as patronizing or dismissive of younger generations' experiences and concerns. The phrase is considered informal and can be seen as disrespectful by some. It reflects a frustration with perceived generational divides and a desire to assert younger perspectives. It is important to acknowledge that using this phrase can contribute to generational stereotyping.

On fleek

On fleek (on fleek) adjective

Describing something that is perfectly done, stylish, or on point, especially eyebrows, makeup, or outfits.

Example: Her eyebrows are on fleek.

"On fleek" gained popularity in the mid-2010s, particularly within online beauty communities. While its usage has decreased somewhat, it is still occasionally used, often ironically or humorously. It emphasizes perfection or flawless execution. Synonyms include "perfect," "flawless," "on point," "stylish," or "looking good." While now considered somewhat dated, its occasional use serves as a reminder of past trends and can be used to create a nostalgic or humorous effect.

Out of pocket

Out of pocket (out uv pok-it) adjective

Describing behavior or actions that are inappropriate, offensive, or beyond the bounds of acceptable social conduct.

Example: That joke he made was totally out of pocket.

"Out of pocket" is a phrase that has been used in various contexts for some time, but its usage within Gen Z is consistent with its established meaning. It implies a violation of social norms or boundaries. Synonyms include "inappropriate," "offensive," "unacceptable," "rude," "disrespectful," or "crossing the line." The use of "out of pocket" often conveys a sense of shock or disapproval. It can also be used to describe actions that are surprising or unexpected, even if not necessarily offensive.

P

Periodt

Periodt (peer-ee-uht) interjection

Used to add emphasis or finality to a statement, indicating that there is no room for argument or further discussion. It's a way of asserting a point definitively.

Example: That's just how it is, periodt.

"Periodt" is an emphatic version of "period," which has been used for some time to add emphasis to a statement. The added "t" intensifies the emphasis and creates a more playful or dramatic effect. It originated within Black Vernacular English (AAVE) and has become widely adopted by Gen Z. It's often used in online communication and social media, particularly in response to opinions or arguments. It signals a strong conviction and a refusal to engage in further debate. Synonyms include "end of discussion," "that's final," "case closed," or "no further questions."

POV

POV (Point Of View) (pee-oh-vee) abbreviation/phrase

An abbreviation for "Point Of View." In its original context, it refers to a camera angle or perspective in film or video. In slang usage, it refers to a specific perspective or scenario, often presented in a video format on platforms like TikTok, where the viewer is placed in a particular situation or role.

Example: POV: You're trying to study, but your roommate is playing loud music.

"POV" is a term borrowed from filmmaking. Its usage in Gen Z slang has evolved to create immersive or relatable scenarios for viewers. POV videos often use first-person perspective to place the viewer directly into the described situation. The term has become a popular way to create engaging and relatable content online. It allows for creative storytelling and the exploration of different perspectives.

Pressed

Pressed (prest) adjective

Used to describe someone who is overly concerned, worried, or bothered by something, often to the point of being stressed or agitated. It can also imply that someone is trying too hard to impress or gain attention.

Example: He's so pressed about what everyone thinks of him.

"Pressed" in this context is a figurative extension of its literal meaning of being squeezed or compressed. It implies a state of being under pressure or stress. It is often used with a slightly negative connotation, suggesting that someone is being overly sensitive or anxious. Synonyms include "stressed," "worried," "anxious," "bothered," "concerned," or "obsessed." The use of "pressed" can also suggest that someone is insecure or trying too hard to validate themselves.

Purr

Purr (pur) interjection/exclamation

Used as an expression of approval, satisfaction, or agreement, often in response to something stylish, attractive, or pleasing. It can also be used to express excitement or anticipation.

Example: That outfit is fire! Purr.

"Purr" is a relatively recent addition to Gen Z slang that has gained popularity on social media. It's a playful and expressive interjection that conveys a positive reaction. The onomatopoeic nature of the word evokes the sound of a cat purring, which is associated with contentment and pleasure. It's often used in response to fashion, beauty, or other forms of self-expression. It can also be used in a more general sense to express approval or excitement. It is similar to other interjections such as "slay," "periodt," or "yass."

Q

Quiet Part Out Loud

Quiet Part Out Loud (kwahy-uht pahrt out loud)
phrase/idiom

Used to describe the act of saying something that is usually kept unspoken or implied, often something controversial, uncomfortable, or socially taboo. It implies that someone has voiced a hidden truth or an unspoken opinion.

Example: He finally said what everyone was thinking; he said the quiet part out loud.

"Quiet part out loud" is a relatively recent phrase that has gained popularity in online discussions and social commentary. It highlights the act of verbalizing something that is typically avoided in polite conversation. It can be used to describe both positive and negative situations, depending on the context. Sometimes, saying the quiet part out loud can lead to greater understanding or resolution, while other times it can cause conflict or offense. The phrase emphasizes the act of bringing something hidden into the open. It implies that the unspoken thought or opinion was widely shared but not openly discussed until someone voiced it.

Quote Retweet

Quote Retweet (often shortened to "RT") (kwoht ree-tweet/ar-tee) noun/verb

1. Noun: A feature on Twitter that allows users to retweet someone else's tweet while adding their own commentary or quote.

2. Verb: To use the quote retweet feature on Twitter.

Example 1 (Noun): I saw a hilarious quote retweet of that viral tweet.

Example 2 (Verb): I'm going to RT this with my own thoughts.

While "retweet" itself is not Gen Z slang, the specific practice of quote retweeting and its abbreviation "RT" are highly relevant to online communication and social media culture, particularly among younger generations. A quote retweet allows users to not only share someone else's content but also to add their own perspective, critique, or commentary. It's a key way to engage in online discussions and debates. The term "RT" is often used interchangeably with "retweet" in informal online communication. Quote retweets can be used for various purposes, such as adding humor, providing context, or expressing disagreement. They are a significant part of how conversations unfold on Twitter and other social media platforms.

R

Ratio

Ratio (ray-shoh) noun/verb

1. Noun: In the context of social media, specifically Twitter, it refers to the disproportionate number of replies or comments a post receives compared to the number of likes or retweets. A high reply-to-like/retweet ratio indicates that the post is unpopular, controversial, or has elicited strong negative reactions.

2. Verb: To receive a high reply-to-like/retweet ratio, indicating that a post has been poorly received.

Example 1 (Noun): That tweet got a massive ratio; everyone was criticizing it.

Example 2 (Verb): He got ratioed for his controversial take.

"Ratio" as social media slang originated on Twitter and has become a widely understood metric for measuring online engagement and public opinion. It's a quick and informal way to assess the reception of a post. A high ratio suggests that the post has struck a nerve, often negatively. It's a very public and visible form of online disapproval. The term is mainly used on platforms where replies are easily visible alongside likes/retweets. It emphasizes the collective response to a post rather than just individual approval.

Real One/Real G

Real One/Real G (reel wuhn/reel jee) noun

Used to describe someone who is genuine, authentic, and loyal. It implies that someone is true to themselves and others, and that they possess integrity and strong character. "Real G" is a more emphatic version of "Real One," with "G" standing for "gangster" but used in a non-violent, metaphorical sense to mean someone respected and authentic.

Example 1 (Real One): She's a real one; she's always there for her friends.

Example 2 (Real G): He's a real G; he always keeps his word.

"Real One" and "Real G" originate from Black Vernacular English (AAVE) and have become widely adopted in mainstream Gen Z slang. They are terms of high praise and respect. They emphasize authenticity, loyalty, and integrity. Synonyms include "genuine," "authentic," "loyal," "trustworthy," "down-to-earth," or "true to themselves." These terms are often used to describe close friends or people who are admired for their character. They emphasize the importance of being true to oneself and others.

Rizz

Rizz (Charisma) (riz) noun

Short for "charisma." Refers to charm, attractiveness, and the ability to attract or impress others, especially romantically. It describes someone who has a natural ability to connect with people and make them feel drawn to them.

Example: He's got so much rizz; he can talk to anyone.

"Rizz" is a relatively recent addition to Gen Z slang. It's a concise way to describe someone's ability to attract romantic or social interest. It emphasizes charm, confidence, and social skills. While similar to "charisma," "charm," "game," or "flirting skills," "rizz" has a more contemporary and informal connotation. It often implies a natural or effortless ability to attract others. It has become particularly popular on platforms like TikTok and other social media platforms where social interactions and relationships are frequently discussed.

S

Slay

Slay (slay) verb/interjection

1. Verb: To do something exceptionally well, to succeed spectacularly, or to impress greatly. Often used in the context of fashion, performance, or personal achievements. It implies a high level of skill, confidence, and impact.

Example: "She slayed that presentation; it was incredibly insightful and engaging."

2. Interjection: An exclamation of praise or approval, expressing admiration for someone's success or accomplishment.

Example: "Slay! That outfit is absolutely stunning."

"Slay" has evolved beyond its literal meaning of killing to signify a powerful and impressive performance. It emphasizes not just success, but doing so with style, confidence, and a certain level of dominance. The term has gained significant traction in online spaces, often used to celebrate achievements, compliment someone's appearance, or express admiration for a particular skill.

Salty

Salty (sawl-tee) adjective

Used to describe someone who is bitter, resentful, or angry, often due to a perceived slight or disappointment. It implies a sour or unpleasant attitude, often stemming from jealousy, envy, or a feeling of being wronged.

Example: "He's still salty about losing the game and keeps bringing it up."

"Salty" is a figurative extension of the literal meaning of being salty, which is unpleasant and unpleasant to taste. It evokes the image of someone who is "sour" or "bitter" in their demeanor. The term often implies a lack of grace or sportsmanship, particularly in competitive situations. It can also be used to describe someone who is easily offended or quick to anger.

Savage

Savage (sav-ij) adjective/noun

1. Adjective: Used to describe someone or something that is brutally honest, witty, or ruthless, often in a humorous or impressive way. It implies a lack of restraint or filter, and the ability to deliver sharp and cutting remarks.

Example: "Her comeback was savage; he didn't know what to say."

2. Noun: A brutally honest, witty, or ruthless remark or action.

Example: "That was a savage burn! I'm still laughing."

"Savage" has evolved from its original meaning to describe something wild or uncontrolled to signify a particular kind of wit and assertiveness. It often implies a confident and unapologetic delivery of sharp observations or comebacks. While sometimes used negatively, it often carries a sense of admiration for someone's quick wit and ability to deliver a cutting remark.

Sheesh

Sheesh (sheesh) interjection

An exclamation of surprise, amazement, annoyance, or exasperation. It can convey a wide range of emotions, from mild surprise to intense frustration.

Example: "Sheesh, did you see the size of that burger?"

"Sheesh" is a versatile interjection that can be used in various situations. It's a more casual and expressive alternative to words like "wow," "geez," or "goodness." The specific meaning and intensity of "sheesh" can vary depending on the context and the speaker's tone of voice. It can be used to express admiration, disbelief, disapproval, or simply to acknowledge something unexpected or noteworthy.

Simp

Simp (simp) noun/verb

1. Noun: A person, typically male, who is excessively attentive and submissive to someone, especially a woman, in hopes of gaining their romantic or sexual attention. Often used with a negative connotation, implying a lack of self-respect or dignity.

Example: "He's such a simp for her; he buys her everything she wants."

2. Verb: To behave in a way that is considered excessively attentive or submissive to someone.

Example: "Stop simping over her; she's not interested."

"Simp" is a term that has gained significant attention in recent years, often used in a critical or mocking manner. It highlights behavior that is perceived as overly eager to please or gain approval, particularly in romantic contexts. The term can be controversial, with some arguing that it is used to shame or criticize men for expressing their feelings or trying to impress someone.

Situationship

Situationship (sich-oo-ay-shuhn-ship) noun

A romantic or sexual relationship that is not clearly defined or committed, often lacking clear boundaries or labels. It describes a situation where two people are involved with each other but avoid defining the nature of their relationship.

Example: "They're in a situationship – they spend time together but aren't officially dating."

"Situationship" is a relatively new term that reflects the evolving landscape of modern dating. It acknowledges the increasing fluidity and complexity of relationships in the digital age. It can refer to a range of situations, from casual hookups to more emotionally involved relationships that lack a formal label.

Skrrt

Skrrt (skurt) interjection/verb

1. Interjection: An onomatopoeic representation of the sound of tires screeching, often used to indicate a quick departure or escape.

Example: "He saw the police and skrrted away in his car."

2. Verb: To leave quickly or abruptly.

Example: "We skrrted out of there as soon as the party got boring."

"Skrrt" is a playful and energetic term that has become popular in hip-hop music and online culture. It's a concise and expressive way to describe a sudden and rapid departure, often with a sense of urgency or excitement. It can also be used humorously to describe a sudden change in direction or a quick shift in conversation.

Slaps

Slaps (slaps) verb

Used to describe something, typically music, that is excellent, enjoyable, or impactful. It implies that something is very good or impressive, often with a strong emotional or physical response.

Example: "This song slaps! It's so catchy."

"Slaps" is a highly positive descriptor, often used in the context of music, movies, or other forms of entertainment. It emphasizes the impact and enjoyment that something provides. Synonyms include "bops," "rocks," "kills it," or "is amazing." The use of "slaps" suggests that something is not just good, but exceptionally good and highly engaging.

Smol

Smol (smohl) adjective

A deliberate misspelling of "small," used to describe something that is cute, tiny, or adorable. It often refers to animals, objects, or even people that are small and endearing.

Example: "Look at that smol puppy! It's so cute."

"Smol" is a common example of internet slang that uses intentional misspellings for emphasis or humor. It's often used in online communities that focus on cute animals, children, or other adorable things. It adds a playful and affectionate tone to the description.

Snack

Snack (snak) noun

Used to describe someone who is physically attractive or desirable. It implies that someone is visually appealing and tempting, like a delicious snack.

Example: "She's a total snack."

"Snack" in this context is a figurative extension of its literal meaning. It's a playful and informal way to compliment someone's appearance. It often implies a casual and appreciative observation of someone's attractiveness.

Snatched

Snatched (snacht) adjective

Describing someone who is looking extremely good, especially in terms of their appearance, makeup, or outfit. It implies a high level of style, confidence, and attractiveness.

Example: "Her makeup is snatched; she looks flawless."

"Snatched" emphasizes a sharp, polished, and put-together appearance. It suggests that someone has achieved a high level of refinement and style. It can also be used to describe something that is perfectly executed or flawlessly done.

Stan

Stan (stan) noun/verb

1. Noun: An extremely enthusiastic and devoted fan.

Example: "She's a huge stan of that K-pop group."

2. Verb: To be an extremely enthusiastic and devoted fan of someone or something.

Example: "I stan this artist so much; I've seen them in concert five times."

"Stan" originates from the Eminem song of the same name, which depicted an obsessive fan. While the original song portrayed a negative and extreme form of fandom, the term has evolved to describe any highly enthusiastic and devoted fan. It can be used positively to describe someone who is passionate and dedicated to their favorite artist, band, or other object of admiration.

Sus

Sus (suhs) adjective

Short for "suspicious." Used to describe something or someone that seems questionable, untrustworthy, or suspicious. It implies a sense of doubt or distrust.

Example: "He's acting really sus; I think he's lying."

"Sus" is a concise and informal way to express suspicion or doubt. It's often used in online interactions and games, where it can be difficult to assess someone's true intentions. The term has gained significant popularity in online gaming communities, where it's used to describe players who may be cheating or acting suspiciously.

Ship

Ship (as in relationship) (ship) verb/noun

1. Verb: To want or support two people to be in a romantic relationship. It expresses a desire for two individuals, whether fictional characters, celebrities, or real-life people, to become a couple. This desire is often based on perceived chemistry, compatibility, or simply a wishful pairing.

Example: "I really ship those two characters together; they have great chemistry."

2. Noun: A desired romantic pairing. The "ship" refers to the imagined or hoped-for relationship between two people. It can also refer to the act of supporting or advocating for that relationship.

Example: "They're my favorite ship in the whole show."

"Ship" is a shortening of "relationship" and originated within online fan communities, particularly those focused on television shows, movies, and books. It's a key term in fan culture and online discussions about fictional and real-life pairings. The term is often used with a sense of enthusiasm and excitement, expressing a strong desire for the pairing to become a reality. "Shipping" can involve creating fan fiction, fan art, or engaging in online discussions about the pairing. While often used in the context of fictional characters, it can also be applied to real people, such as celebrities or social media influencers. The term has become widely adopted by Gen Z and is a common part of online communication and social media interactions. It emphasizes the active role that fans take in imagining and supporting romantic pairings. It also highlights the importance of shared interest and community within online fandoms. The term is generally used in a positive or playful context, expressing support and enthusiasm for the pairing.

T

Tea

Tea (tee) noun

Gossip or news, often of a scandalous or juicy nature. It implies information that is interesting, revealing, or potentially controversial.

Example: "Spill the tea! What happened at the party?"

"Tea" originates from Black drag culture and has become widely adopted in mainstream Gen Z slang. The phrase "spill the tea" means to share gossip or reveal secrets. It's a playful and informal way to request or share information that is considered exciting or intriguing. The term often implies that the information is not widely known or that it could cause a stir. It is commonly used in online communication and social media, particularly in discussions about celebrities, relationships, or social events. The term has also been used in popular culture, further solidifying its place in contemporary slang.

Thirst Trap

Thirst Trap (thurst trap) noun

A photo or video posted on social media that is intentionally designed to be sexually suggestive or to elicit attention and admiration from others. It is often used to attract romantic or sexual interest.

Example: She posted a thirst trap on Instagram, and her DMs are flooded with messages.

"Thirst trap" is a term that has become prevalent with the rise of social media and online self-expression. It acknowledges the strategic use of online content to attract attention. The term often carries a slightly negative connotation, implying that someone is being overly eager or attention-seeking. However, it can also be used playfully or admiringly, depending on the context. The term recognizes the performative nature of online identity and the desire for validation through social media interactions.

Throwing Shade

Throwing Shade (throh-ing sheyd) verb

To make a subtle or indirect insult or criticism, often disguised as a casual remark or observation. It implies a veiled attack or a passive-aggressive comment.

Example: She was throwing shade at me the whole time with her backhanded compliments.

"Throwing shade" originates from Black drag culture and has become widely adopted in mainstream Gen Z slang. It's a colorful and expressive way to describe a form of indirect aggression. The term suggests a subtle or veiled attack, rather than a direct confrontation. It often involves using sarcasm, irony, or subtle digs to undermine or criticize someone. The term is commonly used in online communication and social media, particularly in discussions about interpersonal conflicts or rivalries.

Triggered

Triggered (trig-erd) adjective (Often used ironically)

While "triggered" has its original meaning relating to a psychological response to trauma, it is often used ironically by Gen Z to describe being mildly annoyed, upset, or bothered by something. It is a hyperbolic use of the term.

Example: I'm so triggered by the slow internet today.

The ironic use of "triggered" has become widespread in online communication and social media. It's a way to exaggerate minor annoyances or frustrations for humorous effect. However, it's important to be mindful of the original meaning of the term and to avoid using it in a way that trivializes or disrespects individuals who have experienced trauma. The ironic use of "triggered" can sometimes be seen as insensitive or dismissive of genuine mental health concerns.

TBH

TBH (To Be Honest) (too bee on-ist) abbreviation/phrase/interjection

Used to preface a statement, indicating that the speaker is being honest and truthful, even if the statement might be unpopular or controversial. It's a way to express candor or frankness.

Example: TBH, I didn't really like the ending of the movie.

"TBH" is a common abbreviation used in online communication and text messaging. It's a concise way to introduce a potentially sensitive or controversial opinion. It signals that the speaker is being upfront and honest. Synonyms include "honestly," "frankly," "to be honest," "in all honesty," or "I'll be honest." The use of "TBH" often implies a desire for transparency and authenticity, even if the truth is difficult or uncomfortable.

That's on me

That's on me (thats on mee) phrase

Used to acknowledge one's own responsibility or fault for something. It expresses ownership of a mistake or error.

Example: "I forgot to bring the tickets. That's on me."

"That's on me" is a common phrase in informal English, and its use within Gen Z is consistent with general usage. It's a concise and direct way to take responsibility. Synonyms include "that's my fault," "I'm to blame," "I messed up," or "I take responsibility." The use of "that's on me" often conveys a sense of accountability and willingness to own one's actions. It can also be used to defuse a potentially tense situation by acknowledging one's role in it.

V

Vibe

Vibe (vahyb) noun

A general feeling, atmosphere, or mood that is perceived or experienced in a particular place, situation, or with a particular person. It can refer to a positive or negative feeling, and it often encompasses a combination of sensory and emotional elements.

Example: "This party has a really chill vibe."

"Vibe" is a term that has been used in various contexts for some time, but its usage within Gen Z has become more widespread and nuanced. It's a versatile term that can be used to describe a wide range of experiences, from social gatherings and music to personal interactions and even online spaces. The term often implies a subjective and intuitive understanding of a situation or person. It encompasses not just the explicit elements of a situation but also the unspoken or subtle cues that contribute to the overall feeling. Synonyms include "atmosphere," "mood," "feeling," "aura," or "energy." The phrase "good vibes" is often used to express positive feelings or approval. The term can also be used as a verb, "vibing," to describe enjoying or connecting with something or someone.

Valid

Valid (val-id) adjective

Used to express agreement, approval, or acknowledgment of someone's point of view, feeling, or experience. It implies that something is reasonable, legitimate, or understandable.

Example: "I understand why you're upset; your feelings are completely valid."

"Valid" is a word that has its standard meaning in formal English, but its usage within Gen Z has become more frequent and emphasized. It's a way to affirm someone's perspective or experience, even if one doesn't necessarily share the same view. It's a way to show empathy and understanding. The term often implies a recognition of someone's emotional state or personal experience. Synonyms include "legitimate," "reasonable," "justified," "understandable," "acceptable," or "fair." The use of "valid" often promotes a sense of inclusivity and acceptance by acknowledging the diversity of perspectives and experiences. It can also be used ironically to acknowledge something that is obviously true or self-evident.

W

W (in the chat)

W (in the chat) (dub-yoo in thuh chat) interjection/noun

1. Interjection: Used in online chat or messaging to signify a win, victory, or success. It is a shortened form of "win."

2. Noun: A win, victory, or success.

Example 1 (Interjection): Just finished my final exam! W in the chat!

Example 2 (Noun): That was a huge W for our team.

"W" is a simple and concise way to express positive outcomes in online communication. It's often used in gaming, sports, or other competitive contexts, but it can also be used more generally to celebrate any form of achievement or success. The phrase "in the chat" emphasizes the online context of the expression. It is directly contrasted by "L" for loss. The use of "W" is a quick and efficient way to convey positive sentiment and celebrate accomplishments within online communities.

Woke

Woke (wohk) adjective

Used to describe someone who is aware of and actively attentive to issues of social justice and inequality, particularly those related to race, gender, and sexuality. It implies a critical understanding of systemic oppression and a commitment to social change.

Example: He's very woke about social issues.

"Woke" originated within Black communities and has become widely adopted in mainstream culture. While it initially carried a positive connotation, it has also become a subject of controversy and debate. The term is sometimes used ironically or sarcastically to criticize those who are perceived as being overly focused on social justice or as engaging in performative activism. It is important to be aware of the different ways in which the term is used and the potential for misinterpretation or misuse. The term's meaning has become increasingly complex and contested in recent years.

Wig

Wig (wig) noun/interjection

1. Noun: A hairpiece or artificial hair. (Standard definition, but relevant contextually)

2. Interjection: An exclamation of shock, surprise, or disbelief, often in response to something impressive, surprising, or shocking. The phrase "wig snatched" or "wig flew" is often used to emphasize the level of shock.

Example 1 (Noun): She wore a beautiful wig to the party.

Example 2 (Interjection): That performance was incredible! Wig!

The slang usage of "wig" is a figurative extension of the idea of one's wig being "snatched" or flying off due to intense shock or surprise. It is a hyperbolic expression that conveys a strong emotional reaction. The phrase "wig snatched" or "wig flew" emphasizes the extreme nature of the surprise or shock. It's a very expressive interjection.

Withdrawal

Withdrawal (with-draw-uhl) noun (often used hyperbolically about missing something)

While "withdrawal" has its original meaning relating to the symptoms experienced when stopping the use of a substance or being removed from something one is accustomed to, in Gen Z slang, it is often used hyperbolically to describe missing someone or something intensely. It implies a strong feeling of longing or absence.

Example: I haven't seen my best friend in a week; I'm going through serious withdrawal.

The hyperbolic use of "withdrawal" is a figurative extension of its original meaning. It exaggerates the feeling of missing something or someone, comparing it to the physical and emotional distress associated with substance withdrawal. It's a way to express strong affection or attachment in a humorous or relatable way. It is important to distinguish between this casual usage and the serious medical condition of withdrawal. The hyperbolic use emphasizes the intensity of the longing or missing feeling.

Y

Yeet

Yeet (yeet) interjection/verb

1. Interjection: An exclamation of excitement, surprise, or triumph, often accompanying a throw or forceful movement.

2. Verb: To throw something with force or enthusiasm. It can also mean to move quickly or abruptly.

Example 1 (Interjection): Yeet! I made the basket!

Example 2 (Verb - throwing): He yeeted the ball across the field.

Example 3 (Verb - movement): I yeeted out of there as soon as the meeting ended.

"Yeet" has gained significant popularity in recent years, particularly on platforms like Vine (now defunct) and TikTok. It's a versatile term that can be used in various contexts, from sports and games to everyday situations. The word is often accompanied by a physical action, such as a throw, a jump, or a quick movement. It adds a sense of energy and enthusiasm to the action or exclamation. The term's origins are debated, with some tracing it to African American Vernacular English (AAVE), but its current widespread use is largely attributed to its viral spread online. It is often used humorously or playfully.

Yikes

Yikes (yahyks) interjection

An exclamation of surprise, shock, alarm, or embarrassment. It expresses a feeling of discomfort, awkwardness, or concern.

Example: Yikes, that was an awkward moment.

"Yikes" is an interjection that has been used for some time, but its usage within Gen Z is consistent with established meanings. It's a versatile expression that can be used in response to a wide range of situations, from minor mishaps to more serious problems. It can convey a range of emotions, from mild discomfort to strong disapproval. It is often used in response to online content, such as cringeworthy videos or embarrassing social media posts. The term is often used with a tone of mild dismay or concern. It doesn't have a direct synonym that captures the same range of nuances, but expressions like "oops," "uh oh," "whoa," or "wow" can convey similar feelings depending on the context. It is a very common interjection in online and offline communication.

As we conclude this exploration of American Gen Z slang, we hope you've gained a deeper understanding of this vibrant and ever-evolving aspect of language. We've journeyed through a world of new words, expressions, and cultural nuances, demonstrating how slang reflects the unique experiences and perspectives of today's youth. Understanding this language isn't just about knowing the definitions; it's about bridging generational gaps, fostering better communication, and connecting with a new generation. We sincerely thank you for taking the time to embark on this linguistic adventure with us. If you found this dictionary informative and helpful in your quest to decipher modern slang, we would greatly appreciate it if you could leave a positive review and rating on Amazon. Your feedback not only helps other readers discover this valuable resource but also contributes to the ongoing conversation about language, culture, and the fascinating ways in which we communicate.

www.ingramcontent.com/pod-product-compliance
Lightning Source LLC
Chambersburg PA
CBHW061644250726
48659CB00004B/1367